What Can Swim?

by Michèle Dufresne

Pioneer Valley Educational Press, Inc.

Here is a hippopotamus.
A hippopotamus can swim.

Here is a tiger.
A tiger can swim, too.

Here is a turtle.
A turtle can swim.

Here is a dolphin.
A dolphin can swim, too.

Here is a crocodile.
A crocodile can swim.

crocodile

dolphin

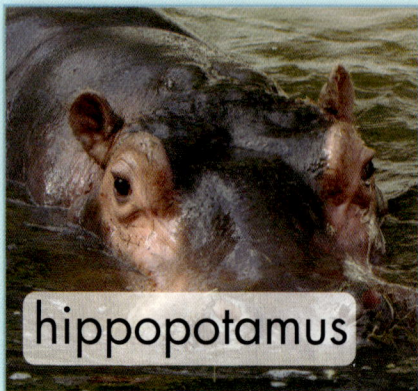

hippopotamus

tiger

turtle